ALL THE MONEY IN THE WORLD

John Menaghan

Salmon poetry

Published in 1999 by
Salmon Publishing Ltd,
Cliffs of Moher, Co. Clare, Ireland
http://www.salmonpoetry.com
email: salpub@iol.ie

© John Menaghan 1999
The moral right of the author has been asserted.

A catalogue record for this book is available from the British Library.

The Arts Council   Salmon Publishing gratefully acknowledges the
An Chomhairle Ealaíon   financial assistance of The Arts Council.

ISBN 1 897648 45 6 Softcover

All rights reserved. No part of this publication may be reproduced or transmitted in any form or by any means, electronic or mechanical, including photography, recording, or any information storage or retrieval system, without permission in writing from the publisher. The book is sold subject to the condition that it shall not, by way of trade or otherwise, be lent, resold or otherwise circulated without the publisher's prior consent in any form of binding or cover other than that in which it is published and without a similar condition, including this condition, being imposed on the subsequent purchaser.

Cover photography & design by Brenda Dermody
Set by Siobhán Hutson
Printed by Techman Ireland Ltd., Dublin

Acknowledgments

Acknowledgement is due to the editors of the following, in which some of the poems in this collection have previously appeared: Poetry Ireland; The Cúirt Journal; California Quarterly; Occident; Berkeley Poetry Review; Salome; Song; Syracuse Poems and Stories; and Stylus.

for my mother

and

in memory of my father

Contents

I.
The Bride of Christ	3
Fire	4
Night Watch	6
Waking to Find You Gone	7
The Fifteenth of February:	
A Breathless Account	8
Wilderness	10
The Prophet of Dream	11
Her Discontent	12
A Lover Turns Contemplative	
in the Absence of Desire	13
Raincoat	14
This	15
Mobile	16
Notes	18
Grief	20
Farewell	21
Frame for a Picture Lost	
in the Memory's Fire	23
The Truth	24

II.
Secrets	29
Bicycle	30
Song	31
Dance	32
Morning	33
Silence	34
Faith	35

Trust	36
Perfection	37
Solitude	39

III.

Central Park West	43
Like A Girl Saying Yes	45
The Midnight Sun Will Never Set	46
Everything You Always Wanted to Know About Sax	48
Harmolodics	49
Bags	50
All the Things Your Mother Never Told You	52
Miles	53
Bassman	55
Saxalone	56

IV.

Mortal Dreams	61
Dementia Congenitalis	66
The Scholar Beachbum	67
Elizabeth Gray	69
Airline Representatives Inform the Next of Kin	70
Fireflakes	71
Fall	72
Seven Point Five	73
Garlic	74
The Dream Called Waking Up	75
October Morning	76
My Father in the Backyard	77
How My Father Would Prefer to be Pictured	79
All the Money in the World	81

I

The Bride of Christ

You are dressed in shades
of winter frost and fire,
skin pale in lounge light.
You are telling me you want
to be a nun. I laugh (good-
naturedly, I think) and say:
'Aha! The Bride of Christ.'

When I press for details
of your sacred calling,
you turn your quiet gaze
upon my fingers, dub them
'artistic,' pause, then
after a long moment add:
'I promise to say more
when we are being serious.'

Your eyes' seraphic glow
ignites my foolish fire.
I cup your marble hands
in mine, and coax you into
one more glass of wine.

Fire

After the blaze of bodies,
flames lashing, licking air,
we look through lingering
smoke for the damage done,
turn to each other, ready
to nurse any blisters, burns.

But the flames flare up
between us once again
as we lie there, feeding
the fire blood and bone
– skin smoking, singed.

Touching fingertips across
that blaze, pulling them back
to rest upon our breasts, we
brand our flesh forever with
each other's fingerprints.

A knowing moves over us
like rolling heat, seeps
through skin: that we are
pledged, perfectly, each
to the other, to the fire,
pledged to feed it little
pieces of ourselves, keep
it alive, stoking the flames
with splinters, yet retain
some fuel forever in reserve.

Know, too, that somewhere
each new conflagration will
be put down in a logbook

kept by the God of Fire,
each tale of splinters
yielded to that flame
read to the God of Love
as they lie alone together
at the end of each long day.

We gaze across the distance
that the flames, uniting us,
yet interpose and blow soft
kisses through the interstices
of that fire, make it flare.
The charmed smoke curls like
halos overhead, hovers a moment,
spins and scatters into air.

Night Watch

The study lamp casts a sash of light
across your cheeks, blushing them to
a deeper ruddiness while you sleep.
A midnight rain stops and starts,
thunderless, barely splashing
as it strikes the screen.

I am studying, alternately,
your face and my book. I run
my hand along the comforter
draping your thighs. My eyes
sting like sores each time
I try to put things together,
make all the elements cohere.

Somewhere in your sleeping skull,
or in the wet world perhaps,
a situation prepares to occur,
events are conspiring to happen.

Bone-dry, roofed from the rain,
I study for a secret test whose
hidden questions rest amid the
blankets, books and lamplight,
keeping my lonely night watch
in the ruddy glow of your room.

Waking to Find You Gone

I peer through morning air.
A book, half-read the night
before, yawns face-up on
the floor, keeps its place
inside the windless room.

Last night you slept in
moonglow, the room a zone
of light around your form.
Not as in this daylight
when the walls glare,
white and worn, but
honey-thick in darkness,
gathered gold. I scurried
in beside you to be warmed.

Without your body by me,
I'm afraid. I simply
can't reach out, raise
up the shade or place
one naked foot upon
the floor, cold grey
tile sticking to my
sole, and feel reborn.
Woman at work, missing
midwife, I roll to
your side of the bed
and sleep away my life.

The Fifteenth of February: A Breathless Account

Four days away
and late for
Valentine's Day
and I've been on
the phone all
morning trying
to put my life
back together,
get things done
and I'm getting
ready to leave
to beg for an
incomplete in
Modernism and
I kneel to kiss
you since you're
sitting in this
big brown chair
and you kiss me
like hello instead
of goodbye and
I'm thinking how
when I get back
we can follow this
up but you say
how'd you like
to be late for
your professor
and I say we'd
have to hurry so

you say well hurry
boy hurry and I
think to myself
the hell with
incompletes then
you're above me
and I remember you
said in your
Valentine's note
how the dawn
is breaking now
you're saying I'd
better get going
so I'm pulling
on my pants when
the record hisses
between tracks and
Billie Holiday's
heart starts
singing Lover,
Come Back to Me
in a voice like
sandpaper dragged
through honey
and you grab me,
pull me back down
where you lie so
I just yell it
right out loud:
'Modernism – fuck it!'
'Never *mind* Modernism,'
you reply, flashing
a wicked smile,
'what about *me?*'

Wilderness

Factory smoke
stack hisses
aluminum into
moonlit air.
Freight rips
silence to shreds
of clatter, steel.
Trains, derailed,
scatter trackless
through your dreams.
Aluminum sparkles
like moondust in
the massy, wood-
brown wilderness
of your hair.

The Prophet of Dream

At dinner last night, you left
your food a moment, let the chicken
lose its heat, butternut squash
steaming into the air, let your
right hand drop to the table
like a witness laying flesh
upon a Bible, swore you'd been here
once before, sat at this table,
had this meal – all in a dream,
3,000 miles from where we sat.

'My God!' was all you said. Then:
'I think I dream the future all
the time and never know that's
what it is till it comes true.
I never knew just why it seemed
so damn familiar, so unreal –
as if I were sleepwalking through
old conversations, phone calls, meals.'

You caught your breath, cheeks flushed
with sudden knowledge, checked my look.
'She who does not understand the future
is condemned to live through it.'
I thought, later, this was what
I should have said, a classic case
of staircase wit. Instead, I
called you 'Kreskin,' let it drop.

And then this morning you awoke,
one cold eye gleaming,
turned on me, and said:
'Last night I dreamed you dead!'

Her Discontent

I know it as a man
knows some cold fact
– that fire burns –
whose skin was never
scoured by blue flame.

I know the name
for each emotion
she endures,
as one knows
terms for flowers
but whose brain
has never steeped
in torrid scent.

For she has leant
me every version
of her pain,
had them returned
by one who
says 'I see,'
as doctors will
when mystified.

I've trained my eyes
to sift her motives
from her moves,
and gone stone blind,
whispering in darkness,
darkly: I know
nothing of her,
this stranger I had
taken for my lover.

A Lover Turns Contemplative
in the Absence of Desire

Dark. Late. The walls thin.
Lovers one room over, moans
filtered through plaster, pipe.
Hard not to listen, not to get
hard himself, but he manages,
lying sleepless by a woman
wrapt in linen, fallow flesh.

The woman conjures demons in
her dreams. Groaning, nights,
she wakes at the ragged edge
of spectral vision, nightgown
soaked in sweat, blinks
the image to a black dissolve.

Mares in the garden stamp,
neighing for riders, snorting
anxious breath into the wind.
The woman acquiesces, succumbs
to incubi, drifts back into
the demons' chill embrace.

Neighs trail off like
whistles from some train
snaking through curves.
An empty mount in the pasture
whinnies once across the dark.

He longs for logs to burn,
hot jazz, exploding stars
 – some species of spontaneous
combustion, form of fire –
pensive in the absence of desire.

Raincoat

I am to you now
just an old raincoat,
stained with wear,
that you save for bad
weather, surrendering
appearances. You slip
it from a shadowed hook,
deep in your clothes-
hound's closet, antique
affection weathered
by the changing winds.

It does enough, and
well enough, for rain.
You lean on it, the
fabricated comfort
of old cloth. It
wraps you still
– soft, dry, tight –
its rustle soothing
as some blandishment.

Hanging on or off you,
there when you need it
and when you don't,
it seems both to thrive
and writhe on half-
benign neglect, hooked
and helpless in the
shadows of your life.

This

'Dying can't be worse than this,' you said.
'I feel as if I'd been turned inside out.'
What could I say, who felt already dead?

'What do two people do who feel like us,
Who can't live with each other or without?
Dying can't be worse than this,' you said.

Outside the window, sunlight scorched the lawn.
I saw myself: a ghost of yellow grass.
What could I say, who felt already dead?

'How did we ever come to this at all?
We love each other. Isn't that enough?
Dying can't be worse than this,' you said.

I cleared my throat in case some words should come.
My tongue, a dry leaf, fluttered, then fell still.
What could I say, who felt already dead?

'The world's just all unraveling in my grasp.
I try to gather strands, and lose the thread.
Dying can't be worse than this,' you said.

You reached for me, thin fingers shivering,
enclosed me in your corpse-cold arms, and wept.
'Dying can't be worse than this,' you said.
What could I say, who felt already dead?

Mobile

Silent, bent birds spin
in a waterfall of flight.
Shadows twirl inside
each other's circles
on the ceiling where
the light suspends
a graduated flock:
small reptilian shapes
yielding to versions
of themselves, larger
at every drop
down the cascade.

Your milky fingers
fashioned paper
in some empty
afternoon when
you sat whirling
bits of rainbow
through your cool,
cat-bitten hands
and left them here
for me to hang.

For months you haven't
managed, maybe cared,
to be in touch – that
phrase for sending
scribbles through
the mail or distant,
thinned out voices
over wire, bloodless
abstracts of our lives.

I contemplate this
trace you've left,
these voiceless birds,
striped flights of colour,
versions of one single,
stark design: sharp
wings, indented beaks,
bright, folded breasts
punctured by string.

Notes

I'm listening to
Ornette Coleman
as I write this
down and the
stark, chaotic
music suits the
ragged mood
your letter's
put me in,
that all too
definite denial
of my final,
doomed appeal
to your emotional
high court.

The horns wail,
shriek and sob
while bass and
drums, insistent
as two children
bent on going
in their contrary
directions, tug
the beat. Yet
we have none,
children I mean,
and now so little
else to show
for wasted years
but phantom scars
in all the hidden
spaces lacerated
by our love.

The sax shoots
barbed shafts
into tender
flesh. Trumpet
bullets stop my
heart again and
again but it
keeps thumping
like the bass
– erratically –
and the drums
send some coded
message I can't
decipher while
your letter's
lying there blue
ink on vellum
striking without
refrain the same
wrong note.

Grief

I'm having an affair
with Grief. And let
me tell you: Grief's
one jealous bitch.
'I saw you with Joy
the other day,'
she says. 'Joy?'
you exclaim. 'Why
Joy's no more than
an acquaintance.'
Does Grief care?
No. She wants
you for herself.

Farewell

> *Love is not love*
> *Which alters when it alteration finds.*

Tonight I walked through January's dark
while midnight tolled on cold carillon bells,
eating an ice-cream cone in fog-filled air,
and thought of you, back now where winter rules
and clouds the breath and chills the marrow bone.

I didn't long for you, yet still recalled
what made me, sometimes, happy when you still
lived with me, loved me still: late evening walks
after time spent together yet alone,
me writing poems out in the living room,
you in the bedroom gobbling someone's prose.

We'd walk out into Berkeley's year-round Spring,
buy ice-cream, stroll to Scenic, cross the grounds
of the Pacific School, perch at its edge,
and gaze on a true panoramic view:
the Bay Bridge, Oakland, San Francisco, all
lit like the Milky Way, off to stage left;
Golden Gate, straight ahead, swathed in grey fog;
Marin's dark hills rolling into Richmond
at stage right. We'd gaze, smile, hold each other
so loosely, absently, content to let
the night pursue its steady course toward dawn.

Tonight, my cone devoured, I turned away
from that same view and felt none of the pain
it lately held. I didn't cry, or call
your name across the land to where you lay,
a continent away, asleep with your

new husband by your side, snug under sheets,
blankets, comforter, and your shared warmth,
soft belly swelled with child new-conceived.
Instead, I found myself singing a tune,
one I'd once tried to sing when you'd first gone.

Back then, I couldn't feel what that song said,
and yet tonight I sang effortlessly:
'No regrets. No tears goodbye. We'd only
cry again, say goodbye again.' Two years,
it's taken me, and more, to mean those words.
And these, the last, perhaps, I'll send to you:
Wherever else you go, whatever do,
– through every change of climate, heart, and mind,
past all imagining, distance, and time –
my love's unaltering: I wish you well.

Frame for a Picture Lost in the Memory's Fire

Somewhere behind my eyes
this sultry night like
satellite transmissions
shattered by the atmosphere
or faces not quite caught in
broken glass, a picture fades,
then flickers, aims at form.

As if the mind were feeble,
not expert at losing or
transmuting into fire each
graven image we would most
preserve, I reassemble
fragments of appendage,
glance, remark. Negatives
fading darker – blackened,
scorched. A phoenix fire?
Nothing arises but ash
drifting over desire.

What is preserved? Words,
framing not a face but
the bitter knowledge
flame engraves; smoke
that lingers, floats
into the loser's throat;
nights like this: no fire
within me, none without.

The Truth

I'm at my brother's
beach house in New Jersey
with the woman I
used to be married to.
At the time, I am married to her.
We're with the man
she's married to now.
At the time, she's not married to him.
We're also with my nephew,
whose parents aren't married anymore.
Well, his mother is, but
not to my brother, right?

Anyway, we're having dinner,
the four of us: me, the woman
I've married, the man she'll
marry later, and my nephew,
too young back then to marry anyone,
and we're talking and laughing
and eating and drinking,
and we've been at the beach
and it's been a good day
and the food tastes great
and everyone's getting my
jokes, or pretending to, so
I say: 'Hey, you know something?
This is the way it's supposed to be.'

So then everybody smiles and nods
 between bites of food and bits
of conversation, and my wife says:
'Really, that's the truth!'
And her future husband just looks

glad to be included in
this odd domestic bliss we've
stumbled into for a day,
while my nephew, doing his best
to seem one of the gang,
tries not to show he's just
a trifle puzzled by the sentiments
his elders have expressed.

That was a while back.
Some things have changed.
What talking, eating, laughing
we do now takes place in
different circumstances, spots.
And yet what we said then
and what we felt, assembled
round that table happily, unheeding
as the last sun caught the day's
last wave and darkness dropped
and the tide turned,
retains, despite such change,
its simple truth.
It's true. The whole truth.
Nothing. But the truth.

II

Secrets

whole civilisations
floating like
icebergs so much
under water so much
lurching through
oceans shedding
its own dark light
hissing ice plunging
through chilly seas
letting currents
carve it cryptically
sun patiently sending
down punishing heat
waiting for cracks
to sound through
frosted air wind
slicing waves into
swells and surges
keening syllables
close to speech

Bicycle

A bicycle waits in the gloom
at the edge of a street while
the fine rain's swift sheer
curtain falls before me where
I stand on a black wrought
iron balcony gazing down into
the damp abandoned street in
the stillness of this sombre
afternoon waiting for a frail
young woman to appear and
pedal slowly towards the sun.

Song

A voice that cannot find its key,
a voice locked out of melody,
it floats upon the air like dust
and settles for what notes it must.

Like pebbles scattered on a drum
it makes its ragged, raucous noise
while other tongues stand silent, poised
– waiting for songs that will not come.

Dance
for Jennifer

You dance against the nothing.
Blink.
And the nothing is still there.

Dance against the darkness.
And the darkness fills the air.

Twirl, spotting, on the cold wood floor
a palpable
absence, wind spinning through your ears.

Blink and twirl. Twirl and blink.
Your body filling, filled with fear.

And when at last the dance ends,
You stand swaying,
eyes combing wood grain, swirling floor.

Eager for nothing. Anxious for still more.
Wanting to know without knowing you want to know

what the darkness is wearing, how
to dance
into the sleek shape of thin air.

Morning

A taste of darkness
lingering in the throat.
Fume fogging glass.
Slim finger scraping
moisture from the pane,
caressing burning lids
with liquid breath.

Silence

What you don't say
about the sunlight
splintering into
sparks, training
your eyes like
weapons on the
glittering bay.

Faith

Not faith
but mystery
moves me
makes me
await what
might be
next around
the corner
of this
spinning sphere
it took
me time
to learn
not to
regret not
knowing what
was true
stop longing
for false
certainty cherish
chaos thrill
to mystery
appreciate at
long last
leaving faith
behind had
meant not
loss but
liberty.

Trust

You know yourself so well you'd be a fool
to trust yourself, and yet you must.
Watch, while you haul your soul
from dust to dust.

Perfection

If you picked out parts
of the world, selected
carefully enough, put them
together in your mind,
you could find perfection.
There, in the mind, but
never in the world. So
that living in a place
where a massive bay kept
things from ever getting
beastly hot or ghastly
cold, where hills rimmed
fertile flatlands, dry
but not too dry, brown
but not too brown, you
longed, involuntarily,
for green, the verdant
fields and emerald
grasses of your youth.

Walking through a winter
of plum blossoms, pink
flames fluttering in
parched air, you thought
of bright leaves burning
in fall forests. When
the blossoms fled their
branches on warm breezes,
some part of you, though
stunned by splendour, saw
deep inside your mind,
against your will, soft
flurries flying sideways

in a frigid wind and
(wonder of all wonders)
missed, unspeakably, that
delicate blankness: cold,
fast-falling, shrouding snow.

Solitude

Solitude's not a state; it's a continent,
a vast space with a single figure in it.
A silk thread Chinese tapestry wherein
some monk sits sheltered from a waterfall
so massive only contemplation can
disclose the small man smiling on a ledge,
legs lotus-crossed, eyes beatifically
gazing into a swift, sheer drapery.
Beyond which, if he wished to, he might glimpse
visions of company, a wider world,
but sees, if he should see, mere water falling;
feels, if he feels at all, an airy moisture
collecting on his skin and coarse brown garments;
hears, if indeed he hears, the water's thunder:
one long, elided consonantal mantra;
smells, suppose he smells, the faintest fragrance
of granite stripped clean by the rush of water
blending in his wide nostrils with the scent
arising from his damp, clinging attire;
and tastes, if taste he does, his stale saliva
mingling with the moist air moving through him
– motionless master of his perfect breathing.

III

Central Park West
for John Coltrane

Stretched against
the skyline, cats
on the stealthy
prowl of Central
Park. High above
the Hudson, sax
describes North
Jersey in late
light, tugboats
on the river
hauling night
into the harbour
and the park.

Trane lays down
new tracks: cops
chasing shadows;
taxis breathing
yellow breeze;
howls echoing
through alleys;
sinuous sirens
cruising streets.

Evening smoulders,
flares: sax
searing air.
Skyline bursts
one long last
strip of crimson.
Fire roams beyond
the land's black edge.

Five notes in slow
succession blow:
the dust of day
lies sprinkled
still with dark.

Like a Girl Saying Yes*
for Bix Biederbecke

You fingered the thing
all wrong, couldn't read
a note. Yet anything
they played, you gave
right back, but twice
as sweet. Repeat, repeat.
Brass phrases slipping
through that horn of
plenty, out of step,
one step ahead.

The cornet shone each
time it met your
lips under the lights.
Possessed by harmonies
no one had heard
you played all night,
the boy from Davenport
they all called Bix.

Why Louis said
the name itself
alone made one
stand up, the very
word. Your lustre
came from where?
No man could guess.
Inventing phrases,
speaking not a word,
sweet cornet like
a woman saying Yes.

Eddie Condon's description of Bix's sound, circa 1922

The Midnight Sun Will Never Set

Saxes plead with the gentle
piano, taking turns,
twin barristers at court,
rehearse their briefs.

The keys, their jury,
blend and sympathise,
yet undermine, cajole
the pleading horns.

Two tenors choir their
set piece, phrase
emotion in the air.

The keys intrude,
soft messengers of no,
the small refusals
of a melody that
will not yield.

The altos soar
to bold address,
dispute the tenors'
case in higher court,
whine where the tenors
murmured, wince
where they sighed.

Piano sounds a cool,
dispassioned riff,
refusing all.

The saxes blend together
shaping all into the honey
of the horn, aglint in
sunlight, bold, forlorn,
work variations, take
the chords out for a stroll,
then catch the thread,
slip through the needle's
eye, explore the deep,
surface and float above
sweet spinet notes,
wrap tight their claim
against the stubborn
core of melody and
rest their case.

Hammers hit glancing blows
on taut, thin strings,
sneak in the last word, 'no,'
piano fluttering pianissimo.

Everything You Always Wanted to Know about Sax

It's Saturday afternoon and I'm reading
and listening to KJAZ when this music
comes through the speakers that's like
nothing I've *ever* heard before so
I drop the novel I've been lost in,
fling my feet over the side of the easy
chair to really listen because really
there isn't any kind of choice so much
is happening on the record whatever
it is with the saxophone sending out
signals from some black hole in a galaxy
nobody's named yet it's so far out there
and the rhythms so goddamn cosmic I'm
losing my grip on the armchair, the earth,
the concept of gravity while the tune
spirals further and further from melody
as if it just had to keep changing to stay
alive when suddenly it's all over and I
hear Bud Spangler breathing 'Wow' through
his microphone and telling us all out
in radioland that was Eric Dolphy back
in his early sixties' wild, experimental
phase so I'm just trying to catch my
breath as I re-enter the atmosphere,
thinking: thank God, thank you, Eric,
and thanks, Bud, for telling me,
bro, because you know I might
almost have been afraid to ask.

Harmolodics
for Ornette Coleman

bass
smothering
beat so
drums can
roam guitars
surfing foam
on a swirling
sea keyboards
coagulating chords
sax slapping
tunes silly
putty in
their hands
Ornette and
the band.

Bags
for Milt Jackson

John, musing, combs
the keyboard, gathers
notes, holding them,
herding chords into
his warm embrace.

                Connie slants forward,
                lost in a forest
                of cymbals, keeping
                the pace, slapping
                sticks against drum
                skins – tender, firm.

                                Percy's thin
                                fingers run in
                                a fretful frenzy,
                                stroking the neck
                                of the smooth
                                dark double-bass:
                                rosewood ballerina
                                perched on one
                                pointed foot in
                                her man's embrace.

But Bags leans
against a column
off to one side,
sticks under
folded arms,
hardly looking on.

        Then   reaching   for   his   sticks,
            spreading   his   arms
                    like   a   bear
    somnambular   after   wintry   sleep
    he   pads   to   the   vibraphone

       raises his weapons high
        over rows of steel,
         lets the mallets
             drop.

    Taut fists flash and flicker,
        a flurry of punches,
         a boxer's jabs.

         The   audience   reels.
  Brushfire   spreads   on   chromatic   steel.

              Bags
              nods
               to
             applause
       wanders back
to the column,
his sleepy lair.

E   c   h   o   e   s

     of
                steel
                            on
                                    fire

drift
          through
                     smoke
                              filled
                                        air.

All the Things Your Mother Never Told You
for Bobby Bradford

Where does it start?
It doesn't start anywhere it just starts.
What happens after that?
A world of noise you've never heard before.
Why should I listen to this?
Because you're lucky enough to be here.
Where is here?
Everywhere you've never been till now.
Well, what's this song about?
All the things you never thought to be.
Where does it stop?
It doesn't stop anywhere it just stops.

Miles

Candle flame
licking
wind.

Trumpet flicking
fire, shivered
light.

Notes float on
smoke: sax singes,
sings.

Guitar pirouettes
in counter-
point.

Drums drift across
time signatures,
desist.

Bass runs beneath:
hidden, streaming
beat.

The night, like
a shy guest,
shrinks

into a fist
of bluish
dark.

One slow
note curls,
spins,

slithers up
my spine, so
cold

it burns, so
high it never
falls.

Bassman

        black
       curled
        bass
        man
        eyes
        full
        of
      sorrow
      cheeks
     streaked
    with joy
  Silk Cut stuck
to one pale lip
so laid back you'd
swear he's falling
 picking notes
  like seeds
   out of a
   nickel
    bag

•

Saxalone

The saxophone player
plays alone, though
the drumsticks blaze
and the bass thuds
down in a scud
of hail, the piano
runs to the edge
of the scale
and the trumpet
spits out its
notes like teeth.

The saxophone player
charges, retreats.
Slamming the door
on harmony, flip-
ping the lock he
pockets the key.
Sleek and gleaming
three times his horn
flaunts the melody,
brassy with scorn.

When he isn't blowing
he stands and frowns,
thin frame swaying
behind the beat.
When the riffs get
wicked he crouches
right down. He's
a fetus wrapped
round a silver
horn. He's a
lion clutching
his lover in heat.

He takes the tune
through lost and
found, arms held
stiff, head bent
down but he
can't keep his
can't keep his
can't keep his
can't keep his
can't keep his
feet on the ground.

IV

Mortal Dreams
(November 22-25, 1963)

22: Crows Circling, Borg's Pond

Overhead, the crows shouting
curses at the air, circling
the woods above treetops, fanning
out over houses in their flight.
High in November dusk, they weave
vanishing circles, lustrous streaks
of black in a whited, frozen sky.

A boy stands at the pond's edge,
watching in twilight thin ice
thicken, claim a further depth.
Chilly currents swirl up from
the surface, steam his breath.

At nine he knows he shouldn't
test the middle with his weight,
but doesn't know why. He'd drown,
of course, that much they've
told him. How? He doesn't know.
He stands way past the whistle
that says: FIVE! IT'S FIVE!
GO HOME! and wonders how
the water feels, so cold you
die (no matter if you swim).

What this boy doesn't know of
those black crows, circumscribing
him in flight, of ice so thin
it cracks to water, chill as
death on childish skin, he knows.

Understands nothing and still
knows: a nothing sharp and cold.
He dares himself the journey one
last time, out onto the middle
of the pond. The crows' harsh
cries rebuke his childish fear,
send mockery through the skies.

He heads for home in trouble,
sends his shiver through the air,
moves with a thing to tell
when he arrives. When he arrives,
the President's been shot
in some hot state, and no one
listens to his dark, cold fear.

23: Two Football Games

I.
A nation shocked; the boy plays football.
Touch, like every Saturday. The coach
says nothing, runs the same plays, guards
his first-place prospects, won't say die.
November's thin sun. Air so cold
it hurts. The boy blocks, rushes,
wonders if he's 'glad to be alive.'

II.
The newspaper carries pictures
of the clan: 'Those Kennedys.'
Hyannis, playing football
on the beach, in summer,
just before the final race.
And edged in black this
dead man's handsome face.

24: Live Murder

Commie in a crowd of cowboy hats.
The camera tracks him, till a man
steps in, obscures the frame.
A pistol spitting sparks. Lee
Harvey Oswald bites the concrete,
glitters blood among the dust:
a picture that goes out on every set.

The boy calls to his family: 'Hurry!
Watch! Oswald's been shot!' What?
The family circles him in disbelief.
Dallas cops hiss curses through clenched teeth.
The boy stands trembling with a sudden chill,
lost for breath, dull terror in his eyes.
The camera zeroes in on Ruby's kill:
Oswald's face contorted in surprise.

25: T.V. Burial

I.
Four days. Think. The world
was made in seven. The boy
assumes John Kennedy's in heaven.
Living room: funeral passing
on the screen. With mother,
sisters, brother the boy watches
little John-John raise his hand
in dumb salute to his dead Dad.

He thinks of Grandma dead last
May, when he was eight and barely
understood that she was gone

– or what that meant. Afterwards,
adults all crying at the graveside,
laughing, drinking back at the house.

He starts to cry when John-John
doesn't, starts to comprehend
the bullet's work: cold steel
bursting to blazes in the brain.
His mother says: 'Don't watch.
You needn't. Not if it makes you
cry. Go play.' Play? No games
find lodging in his head. Kennedy,
Grandma and Pope John all dead.

II.
Dinnertime. Death
on every hungry
lip: murdered meat;
potatoes ripped
from earth and
baked alive; limp
spinach green
as slime. *The
pond! The pond!*

The boy pales, sways
in his seat, feels
food climb up his
throat, crawl to
his lips, splash
across the plate.
Mother scolding,
Father frowning
till he drops
dead in a faint.

And later wakes,
alone in bed,
room gone dark.
He screams so
high no sound
comes from his
throat, and then
he's sure he's
dead. His mother
enters to adjust
his blankets,
smooth his spread.

III.
Adrift in darkness.
Silence. Then
a distant whirr
of wings. He
slips to sleep,
steps deeper into
dream, patrols the
pond's black edge.

Bedroom door creaks
open; light crawls
in. Gigantic shadows
brood above his bed.
Parents bend to soothe
their fevered child.
Sunlight, ice, a crack!
The crows descend.

Dementia Congenitalis

'He moves, like morning, through a bright beginning.
moves in a light unfiltered by dull years.
What does he know of evil or of sinning,

'this child striding in sunlight? Oh, what fears
can this lithe-limbed youth feel in his gladness?
He moves, like morning, through a bright beginning.'

But that is the old man's vision, the view from years.
This child walks in a quick and secret sadness.
What does he know of evil or of sinning?

Nothing but witches whispering in his ears,
untold urges, dreams of jagged darkness.
He moves like morning through his bright beginning:

Dawn rides him like a halo till he rears,
coltish, skittish, flexed against surging madness.
What does he know of evil or of sinning?

Only a mind that rises in the skull, tears
at bone walls cased in child's flesh.
He moves like morning through his bright beginning,

waits for the nova flash, exploding sphere:
slivers of starfire blaze on shoulders of air. Yes!
O yes! He knows the devil, a leopard grinning,
who moves thru morning towards his bright beginning.

The Scholar Beachbum: A Letter

Traces of ocean
glisten on bronze
limbs. Sand drifts
over leg hairs.
Ten, or so, of
another morning.
I am dressed to go
nowhere, parked
in a silver chaise,
idly brilliant in
sunlight. They
will never find me.
I am gone for good.
Each week, dear
friend, you forward
royalties to punctuate
the swirl of balmy
days. Your letters
are my only clock.

No one gets out
of high school
without reading
my book. 'It
captures adolescent
agony in adult
prose,' one critic
claims. I defer.
I only know it
sells, how much
it costs, and that
the genius was
to write it young.

Days pass how they
will. I consult
my picnic basket
for diversions.
I breathe the salt
spray, inventing
nothing, neither
fictions nor facts.
They would like me
to come back and
'mature as an artist.'
Tell them I am beached,
brain-scorched with
exposure, facing
the deep, adrift
and out of reach.

Elizabeth Gray

Sometime in the summer of 1711, French Prophets heard rumours that John Lacy would do 'some great things.' Followers learned by the New Year that he had received a divine command to leave his wife and sleep with Elizabeth Gray.
  – Hillel Schwartz, *The French Prophets*

I take the hard will of the universe between
my thighs. I prayed
for this so long. My throat too dry to sound

the words, I whispered litanies of lust.
He came to me at dawn,
spoke forth the order sent to him in dream:

his wife, my husband left outside God's plan.
His face above me flushed,
twin crucifixes tangling at my throat

while we make future prophets for Our Lord,
camisole pushed up above
my breasts, cold beads clutched in one fist,

and all His grace assaulting me with love.

Airline Representatives Inform the Next of Kin

Kneeling in December's dark,
heaving in the bitter breeze,
the lover of the dead man spills
her grief across the patio.

Inside the cozy kitchenette,
its yellow doorway dripping light,
an aqua blue receiver hangs
spinning just above the tile,
forming in its plastic throat
a shrill screech of abandonment.

Outside the woman trembles, weeps
beyond the porch light's beam.
The dead man's children, unaware,
go drifting through their dreams.

Fireflakes

Bloodworms fry on
asphalt, dissolving
into mist: scarlet
gases shimmer up
the air. Spider
strands lace hinges
on a rusty chaise.
Red-faced, blue-eyed,
white-bearded, the
old Communist waits
for a late revolution
like some station master
sunning, expecting one
more train, waits for
this supercharged air
to flake into fire,
motionless but for
a shaping of lips.
Dusty spittle sizzles
on black pitch.

Fall

First the sheer drop down fifty feet or more,
unimpeded flow, scarcely touching rock face,
till it comes to a ridge full of niches that
catch the cascades and make forty tiny falls,
then the cleft where spray has cracked open
granite and mosses grow at the edge of a dark
moist cave where no one goes; further down,
water spreading, losing a little speed, wider
on the rock, sending tiny tributaries off
to the sides you don't even see till you've
stood there and stared, till the spectacle
of it all starts wearing off, and your eyes
wander to the edges; then the splash, thin
white line wavering over a dusky pool,
behind it another cleft, wider this time
and wetter, where gravel and stones gleam,
spray smoking off the pool and a trickle
moving past boulders, making its way down
to its next drop, wider waterfall, through
a brook running wild over withered rocks,
whispering, roaring around a log or two,
frothing into a darker pool where everything
stops – or seems to till you look close and
find water snaking softly off to the side,
flowing through a litter of bright autumn
leaves, under the scenic route, parking lot,
train tracks, freeway, and a frontage road
to the Columbia River, at Multnomah Falls.

Seven Point Five

Boom. The room shivers
one split second. I glance
from book to ceiling, thinking:
What did they drop up there?

The shiver stops. I go back
to my book, but it starts
shaking. The couch slides
as I swing my feet out
toward the buckling floor.
A hurricane lamp drops
five feet as I fall.

I stumble to the bedroom
doorframe, call out:
'Susan!' But she's
frozen, watching windows
splinter, shards cutting
scalloped patterns through
the air. 'Come here!
Come here!' But she just
turns to me, and stares.

I'm screaming when
she shakes me, makes
me loose my grip on
the mattress, free my
fingers from her hair.

Six in the morning.
Sunny California.
Still, bright air.

Garlic

Bulbous, bulging clove of ashen white,
it strips to red, and then to white again:
pungent striptease, fragrant nakedness.

You take one moist pit shape and lay it down
beneath a blade – pound, pound – and watch the shards
oozing cellophane blood, viscous and sheer.

Bubbling in oil, dancing like a bride
caught in the frenzied flame of legal lust,
it scents the room with rumours of disgrace.

Lingering in your blood and on your breath,
it lets you deck a man, hands at your sides,
standing still, just breathing face to face.

Alone and meditative two days hence,
you'll raise a hand to prop your weary head,
and that stale smell will seep into your brain,

that tiny pit send out its potent scent
– a hunger rising in your stomach then,
a meal of memory stirring on your tongue.

The Dream Called Waking Up

knife blade
glinting pale
fist flashing
inches from
shut eyes
like flaps
of resealed
envelopes
viscid lids
rise wet
windows
trilled by
lightning
dark as
pitch singed
throat raging
sockets fingers
fumbling for
the switch

October Morning

This pond becomes a skating rink in winter;
today the sun shines down on tepid water.
A flock of Canada geese sits on the pond,
unmirrored in the blaze of morning light.

Suddenly a motion halves the air.
Wings flutter, flap. Birds vault
into the sky, attain their
cruising height and form a V.

One lone bird honks, remains
upon the water, calls his flock
to find him, to discover what they
lack. They arc wide, circle back

to pass above the water where he honks.
He sights them like a target, scales the air,
his shadow widening, paling on the pond,
honks and honks and spends his every stroke

to catch them, match their speed, but
they are gone. He circles now, alone
above the pond, then skids into the water.
Whether he mourns for his lost mate,

or for the sight of all with whom he's flown,
or not at all, but honks like any ship's horn
in a fog, one cannot know. Only that when
he flaps his wings to scatter water,

tilts his head back, sounds his piercing cry,
he gazes at a clear, bright, vacant sky.

My Father in the Backyard

Each summer night he is
the same. Some nights
are clear. Others,
it may rain. The dark
settles in, and so does
my father, straight-
backed in a wooden lawn
chair – wooden, immobile.
Vacant eyes directed
toward a dim horizon.

Some nights he sleeps.
Others, merely shuts
his eyes for a time.
He does not mind
if you sit by him,
or even if you talk.
He will answer questions
(after a fashion) but
never ask you any.

He sits in the yard,
his back to the house,
smoking a twenty-five-
cent cigarillo with
mild deliberation.

He can always outlast
you. On clear nights,
bothered by bugs, you
retreat to the house,
urging him to follow.
If pressed, he'll explain

how mosquitoes come and go,
absenting themselves as
the evening progresses.

If it rains, he predicts
a brief shower, taking
cover under the umbrella:
solemn smoker curtained
by a surround of rain.

When at last he enters
the house, sometimes
slightly wet, but most
times dry, he'll settle
down with the newspaper,
read it through to the
soundtrack of t.v. blare.

No point to inquire.
He'll never admit he's
been thinking a thing.

How My Father Would Prefer to be Pictured

Let the cigars
cost a buck a piece.
Picture me in
a Norfolk jacket,
rosewood chair.
Hunched shoulders;
aristocratic slouch.

I talk to those
who come and go,
yet hold myself
aloof, the proper,
thoughtful distance
of a thinking man.

Let it be morning,
the sole shower
consisting of
dappled light.

For those tasteless
mosquitoes let us
substitute, well,
butterflies –
alighting on my
browned shoulders
as if I were the
new Saint Francis.

Let me be ever
alert, surveying
the landscape,

watchful eyes
seizing each
pulsing sight.

Let my clever son
kneel at my left hand,
my steady, artful
fingers stroking
his submissive head.
Let him not know
how to read or write.

All the Money in the World
(for R.V.M., 1954-1980)

Four thousand miles from the last place
I saw you alive, a drunken young girl
on a London double-decker in Camden Town
who's spent the last five minutes mouthing off
at everyone and everything she sees
suddenly cracks the window at her high perch
and shouts at the top of her range to someone below:
'Ray! . . . Murphy! . . . Ray, you fucker! . . .
Murphy! . . . Ray! . . . Hey, *Mu*rphy! . . . Ray!'
It takes every last shred of sense I've got
not to look down, hoping to find you there.

I cruise a record shop for cheap cassettes
and find Ry Cooder's *Paradise and Lunch.*
It looks familiar somehow; I recall hearing it.
So I buy it, take it home, play it all night.
Until it comes to me you'd owned the disc and
suddenly I'm missing you unspeakably while Ry
sings 'Ditty Wa Ditty' or 'Fool About a Cigarette.'

In the mail this morning a note from my mother
reminding me it's five long years you're dead.
That means you're gone nearly as long as I knew you,
choked on poison fumes when a Camel slipped
from your callused, weed-stained grip in
New Orleans, conked out on the couch as it
smouldered to flame. They found you dead
beneath the bathroom window – smoke, not burns.

I could say you were just a fool for a cigarette,
or hope you're having lunch in some paradise.
Instead, I fill a tumbler with Jameson's,
listening as Ry sings a chorus you used to love:

> *Feelin' good, Feelin' good*
> *All the money in the world*
> *Spent on feelin' good*

I let this *Uisce Beatha*, water of life,
coat my throat with its warm, deceptive glow
and echo that girl in a whiskey-hoarse whisper:
Ray . . . Murphy . . . Ray, you fucker . . .
Murphy . . . Ray . . . Hey, Murphy . . . Ray